Catherine Prender

Can I Use I?

Because I Hate, Hate, *Hate* College Writing

By Catherine Prendergast
with pictures by Hann Lindahl

First published in the United States by Out of Pocket Press

Printed by CreateSpace

First Edition: March 2015

For the kid

Table of Contents

 **Intro**

It's okay. You're going to get through this. And it's going to be easier than you thought.

Everyone has some anxiety when it comes to writing college papers. Everyone wants to know if they're doing this thing right. Most of the questions you have, everyone in your class has. I know because I've heard the same questions in composition classes I've taught or observed over the last few decades.

Maybe you don't think you're a good writer. Don't worry about that. Good writing is your writing. You'll write best by putting yourself in every page. Never forget, you were a person before you were a student. You're still that person. Write like that person. Write like your instructor is also a person. It will help.

Read this book front to back, or read only the sections you need. Read it screaming, cursing, or laughing if you want. Leave it in a coffeehouse, in the bathroom, in a bar, or burn it when you're done. And, when you're losing your mind

1

because you have a paper due and you don't know where to begin, remember, it's just a paper. Someday, your college writing class will be a distant memory, and you'll be on to better things. It will all work out. You are going to get through this, and I'll do my best to help.

What If I Don't Understand My Assignment?

They say that the decisions emergency responders make in their first five minutes at the scene are the most critical. It is in those first five minutes that firefighters and paramedics find out what they don't know: the size of the blaze, what injuries are life threatening, how close the nearest hospital or backup fire station are. When you are handed an assignment, it's not burning up or bleeding from the jugular; nevertheless, what you find out in the first five minutes of getting the assignment can save your paper from developing more serious problems later on.

Consider your writing assignment an emergency that needs immediate attention. You can start working on it the moment your instructor hands it to you. Before you even leave the classroom, you can set to work on that assignment by reading it over carefully. If there's anything on that assignment sheet you don't understand, you can't afford to wait even a few days to find out what it is. If you're going to need help, you need to know that now.

Stress over Time

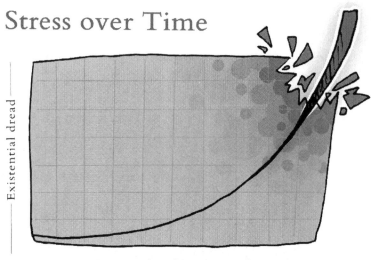

Existential dread

Time as paper due date approaches

No instructor, no matter how good, puts everything they're thinking onto the assignment sheet. And no student, no matter how well prepared, feels completely confident when facing a new writing challenge. Every assignment, from the thoroughly detailed to the open and sketchy, presents puzzles. What you need to complete your assignment is not more brains—you have enough—but clarity. And there are a few simple steps you can take to get it:

First, read the assignment. Read every line—not just the due date. Then, read it three more times.

As you read the assignment, take notes on it, just as you would on a textbook chapter. Write questions in the margins. Underline words you don't understand.

Listen to what the instructor says as the assignment is handed out. Often instructors verbally explain the "big picture" of how the assignment fits into the course. Understanding what you're supposed to learn from writing the paper will help you complete it successfully.

Also in their verbal comments, instructors often give examples of what they "don't" want to see in papers. If you don't easily see the difference between what they "don't" want to see and what they "do" want to see, ask for more explanation.

The due date gives you a clue as to how much work you should be putting into a paper. Is the paper due in two weeks? It probably shouldn't be started the night before it is due. If your instructor thought that you could do the assignment overnight, they would have made the due date the next day.

Make a list of resources you will need to write the paper. Does it call for you to consult course readings? Go to the library? Interview someone? Make an estimate of how much time it will take you to gather whatever resources you need.

Are citations required? Has your instructor given other specific formatting guidelines? Is all the information you need to meet such requirements readily available?

Is your assignment really a sequence of mini–assignments? Has your instructor specified draft due dates or peer review dates or given other signs that your paper will be constructed in pieces over time?

Finally—and this is most important—force yourself to ask your instructor at least one question about the assignment. Why? It gives you a chance to get to know the instructor and gives them a chance to get to know you. Your instructor will notice that you read the assignment—always a plus.

Why do all this in the first five minutes, and not later? Instructors do not love an email inbox full of student questions the night before a paper is due. If an instructor even suspected any students of procrastinating, an email within hours of the due date is a dead giveaway. You'll have plenty of time to ask follow-up questions if you ask your first on day one.

What Should I Write About?

Your college writing instructor would rather not have to read a paper on the following topics: abortion, capital punishment, euthanasia, global warming, gun control.

College writing classrooms (and dinner parties) are no place for these topics. Experienced composition instructors will often forbid one or more of them, for one of any of these reasons: They fear that students have already made up their minds about these issues long ago, so research will only be conducted to confirm unshakable opinion; they know that a search through a library database on the term "global warming" will yield an obscene number of entries (don't even try to Google it); they suspect any topic where the discussion boils down to "for" and "against"; they worry their students will spend most of their time wondering if their instructor is "for" or "against" instead of writing the paper. Finally, they are just plain sick of these topics and feel dry heaves coming on every time they're mentioned.

All of the above are good reasons to avoid writing about abortion, capital punishment, euthanasia, global warming, and gun control. The best reason to avoid these topics, however, is that they're topics, and when you're striving to write a great college paper, having a topic doesn't help you much.

I know how crazy that sounds. It does seem at times that the college writing classroom is all about finding a topic. Brainstorming activities invite you to cluster or map your way to a topic. "What's your topic?" will be the first question the librarian asks when you go off in search of materials. Your instructor in conference might respond to your verbal description of your plans by affirming, "Great topic!"—by which they mean, "Thank goodness this one's not writing about euthanasia."

Likely, though, your instructor will want to hear more. They may ask, "What interests you about that topic?" by which they also mean, "What should interest anyone about that topic?" They're not looking for a topic; they're looking for a reason to care.

The truth is this: Just because everyone is talking about a controversial topic doesn't mean people actually care about it. Of course we all "care" about global warming, those of us who pay attention enough to believe in it, anyway. But we care in the abstract. We care in the way that we know we should care, because we are all subject to its relentless march. We care because we feel guilty, but we also feel guilty that we haven't called our parents in a week. The next time we pick up the phone, however, we're calling our friends. I care about global warming. I think about it a lot while I'm driving my car. But true caring hits closer to home than climate change for most people.

When you're looking for a place to start writing, think less about controversial topics and more about caring questions. The best questions come from wanting to make life a little less difficult, for someone. They force us to rethink what we thought was obvious and ask us to come up with alternatives. Or, they bring to our attention what we never considered important. Instead of asking us to weigh the pros and cons of belief in global warming, for example, a paper could ask how scientists who research climate change negotiate political pressure in their applications for grant funding. Whether you believe in global warming or not, that question still matters.

For practice, go ahead and write down questions that are less about right and wrong, and more about how or why. Then, pick one that you want to answer, because you care about it. Find a question that drives you, that will keep you motivated when you think you're the only one awake at 3 a.m.

But make sure that you're ready to learn. If your question is just your dead–set opinion rephrased, it's not a good question for a college class. A fundamental premise of research is that new information can lead to new beliefs about the world, and, from there, to beneficial action. It's okay to have a hunch, but you shouldn't know the answer to your question before you start. A paper that doesn't surprise you won't surprise anyone else. If you were certain of your thesis when you started the paper, you weren't genuinely asking a question, were you?

In writing, we ask questions of the world, but inevitably the answers we get are about us and what we value. Ideally, your time in a college writing classroom should allow you to set aside your opinions just long enough to ask yourself why you have them.

How Is College Writing Different?

The funny thing about the five–paragraph essay is that nobody likes it, but nobody can kill it. Teachers hate it, but they have to teach it because it helps their students succeed on standardized tests that are used to assess their school's performance. Standardized test designers hate it because it games the system, producing too much of a standardized response. But nobody hates the five–paragraph essay more than composition instructors who have to un–teach it so that their students can learn how to write a college paper.

You probably already know how it goes: You begin with your introductory paragraph, punctuated by a thesis, proceed to three body paragraphs that give supporting points in order of strength, and end with a conclusion that restates the thesis and offers a concluding remark. Did mastering this teach you skills you might use in college? Some. But that doesn't mean you should keep using it. Trying to write a college–level paper in five paragraphs is like trying to balance the chassis of an SUV on training wheels.

Why does the five–paragraph essay fail to work in college? It generally contains little to no research. It has no clear audience. It presents complex problems as though they were simple. It says nothing new, and it says it more than once.

So how do you kick the habit of writing in five paragraphs? Write a sixth paragraph.

This is not another body paragraph that adds one more point to support the thesis. This is the paragraph that takes you beyond CNN–style talking points on the issue into something new. In that sixth paragraph you pull out one point, and one point only, from your former five–paragraph essay, and start writing an entire paper about it.

For example, if your five–paragraph essay is on how you stopped going to the cinema because it's better to watch movies at home, you might re–examine your point that movie theater behavior has become distracting, with patrons checking cell phones and teenagers making out in the back row.

It might be distracting to you. It would be distracting to me. But what hard evidence do we have that watching a movie in a cinema is any more distracting than watching a movie at home, where the doorbell can ring, siblings can come in arguing, or the Internet can crash, freezing the Netflix stream?

Next imagine a skeptical reader of your paper: Who would most readily challenge your point that movie theater behavior is too distracting? Maybe teenagers enjoy making out. Maybe someone is on their phone to share details of the movie on social networking sites. One person's annoying distraction is another person's enhanced experience.

Change your question. Instead of asking yourself why you have stopped going to the movie theater, ask why it is that so many people continue to go. Why do people sit through previews and now commercials, only to place themselves one hundred feet and several knees from the nearest bathroom? Why do this when they could watch virtually any movie they want for much less money at home?

That "sixth paragraph" takes you that extra mile. Make that sixth paragraph your first one, and you're on your way to a great paper.

What Makes a Good Research Question?

"How can we cure cancer?" or "How did the universe begin—really?" These are the questions that six-year-olds ask, and keep asking when they become professors. But when those professors sit down to do research, they don't ask those questions. They whittle away at those big questions until they are left with something they can manage. Half the battle in starting a research paper is recognizing an unanswerable question, and not trying to answer it.

I learned this one when I wasn't writing.

On my fortieth birthday I followed the advice of all magazines targeted to women over forty (which, like a typical overachiever, I'd started reading at age thirty–nine) and decided to take up a new sport, something that would give my dwindling years new meaning, stall the ravages of time on my weakening frame, and make me feel "empowered." I was torn between surfing and tennis. Looking around at the midwestern landscape, I realized that unless I could learn to surf on oceans of corn, a racquet was a better investment than a board.

My tennis coach had everything the magazines told me a forty–year–old woman would need for a journey to rejuvenation. The man looked like a young Ryan Gosling. He also proved to be surprisingly good at tennis. A great believer in learning by doing, Sven (let's call him Sven) would feed me upwards of fifty balls while counting the number of serves I managed to hit in out of the number I'd been fed: "One of two, one of three, two of four—back on track for 50 percent." But he also introduced me to a concept that has become critical to me for starting research projects off right—"the Toss."

A Good Toss, if you're a beginner in tennis, goes more or less straight up and down, falling, if you did nothing to interrupt it on its course, just over the baseline in front of you, not too far out that you have to lean way over to hit it, and certainly not behind your back. Seeing me arch painfully backwards to smack a ball clearly beyond my reach, Sven would advise, "Don't hit the bad tosses." Sven managed to be both direct and kind, though he occasionally had the pained look of someone mulling over what fate had led him to shepherding middle–aged women through their first serves instead of making the pro tour.

Sven, I could see, was laboring to find something to praise watching serve after serve go awry. For a long time it was merely my ability to recognize a Bad Toss. Watching me finally catch, rather than try to hit, a ball I threw over my back shoulder, he affirmed: "That's right. Don't hit those bad tosses." And then there was that magic day where I threw a ball up in the air, straight up. I was getting ready to nail it just off its peak when, before I even made contact, Sven said, "That one is going in." He could tell it was going in, he said, just by the toss.

Starting a research paper is similar to learning to serve. You have to spend more time than you think on the question that drives your paper—the Toss, as it were, of all else that will follow. And it is here where a Good Toss can make all the difference in where your paper is going to land.

Let's say you start off with a question like, "How does sexism influence the media in their coverage of women running for public office?" You have the problem that "the media" could be anything: TV, radio, newspapers, magazines, billboards—all are included in the media. This question is the Bad Toss so far over your head you can't hit it.

A better approach may be to say something profound about something modest—perhaps about the portrayal of one particular female politician by two different newspapers.

Maybe your question is too easy. If the answer to your research question can be Googled, it's like a too low toss—it's not even going to get you over the net.

As Sven says, don't even try to hit a Bad Toss. You're better off working with your instructor to find your Good Toss—your just-right research question—before you go further.

Sure, lots of things could go wrong with a Good Toss. You could trip over your shoelace. You could do something funky with your racquet. You could pull an abdominal muscle while swinging. It's on you to follow through, in tennis as in writing, and not screw up. But starting badly can only end badly.

In my second year of tennis instruction I took lessons from a beefy woman who, just months before joining the club, had thwacked her way to the top of the NCAA women's rankings. (Sven had since moved to Northern California to live in a yurt and play in a Dave Matthews tribute band.) Unwilling to even pretend interest in my story of mid–life rejuvenation, she fed me ball after ball in alternating cross–court style, making me run the baseline until I could feel my age in my knees. On our first lesson on serves I tossed the ball up, excited to show off what I had learned … and then banged it into the net. "That toss," she said. "It's just so important."

Yes, it is.

I Hate My Composition Teacher. Can I Switch Sections?

I hated my composition teacher. And I was sure she hated me.

I thought she—let's call her Stacy—was an idiot. Her assignment for us in the second week was to write an essay extolling or condemning a fruit. I'm not kidding. I decided to write about the grapefruit. I recall I had a strong thesis: "The grapefruit is a shameful waste of money."

My evidence was airtight, including an analysis of juice to pulp ratio. Stacy returned the paper with a red line right through "is" in my thesis, revising it to read: "The grapefruit shamefully wastes money." Grade: C−.

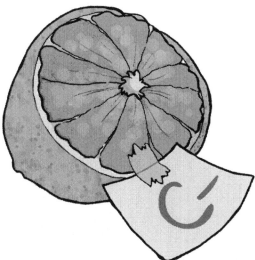

I was distraught. It wasn't the grade—okay, it was totally the grade—but my pride was hurt. I had come to like that essay in the process of writing it. You asked me to write about a flipping piece of fruit, I thought, and I nailed it.

I took my red–lined essay and teenage angst to my father who, with a parent's misplaced desire to make their kid stop crying, assured me my version of the thesis was better than Stacy's: "This makes it sound as though the grapefruit is walking up and down the street, tossing money around." Next to Stacy's correction he drew a really cute plump grapefruit with legs, arms, eyes, ears, and a fedora, walking down the street throwing twenty–dollar bills in the air. We laughed, I stopped sniffling, and then we went out for ice cream.

Because I loved my father, but not my composition instructor, I told Stacy she was wrong about the grapefruit at our next student–teacher conference. I even showed her my father's illustration. She was not so amused. "You've got a real attitude problem," she told me. "You think you're hot shit. I thought I was hot shit when I scored 1580 on my SATs and got into Yale when I was sixteen."

She went on, but I didn't hear the rest. I was thinking, did my teacher really say "shit"? Did my teacher really tell me her SAT scores? Does going to Yale make everyone miserable?

In the weeks that followed, I stopped seeing Stacy as my torturer and started seeing her as a human being. And I could tell her life was no picnic. The class, which met at 8 a.m., was full of engineers who spent the five minutes before she arrived making fun of her squeaky voice—mockery she no doubt overheard. She was a graduate teaching assistant, which meant she had to balance reading our papers with studying for her doctorate in Victorian poetry. She was earning next to nothing for this, so she probably lived on ramen noodles and broth. And, if she still remembered her SAT scores, she was fresh out of college. She was new at this, feeling her way and having to stumble before an audience of twenty jerks, including me.

I kept my mouth shut in class for the rest of the term. In truth, I now knew our instructor was teetering on the brink and might go over with the slightest push. I didn't want to see that. Nobody does. I earned, through several long nights, one of only two A's in the class. I learned a lot about writing—about diligence—by taking the grapefruit-sized chip off my shoulder. I found I could get the most out of every assignment by treating it as a professional writing challenge, as if a movie producer had called me up and barked into the phone: "I need five jokes about a carrot. Yesterday!"

I also learned invaluable lessons by observing what didn't work—observations that I kept to myself. I learned never to tell students they had attitude problems or to ask them to write about fruit. This would help me when I, not too many years later, would be that clueless new teacher in front of a room full of students with attitude problems.

I learned Stacy was right about me: I was too often the smartass student, sure I knew more than my teachers. Looking back, I wish I had been nicer, not just for the good karma, but because compassionate writers are better writers. They are compassionate enough with themselves to allow the long and imperfect process that is writing to run its course. They are good academic writers because they can set aside their judgments long enough to consider that every story sounds good when you hear only one side.

So what do you do when you do not love your composition class? You learn anyway.

Where Do I Start My Research?

No matter what you're going to write about, your research begins in your classroom. The syllabus the instructor hands you is one of the most important sources that you will need to write your paper. Most people pay attention to the numbers on the syllabus: due date, number of pages required, office hours of the instructor. But take a moment to look past the numbers.

Most people read the paragraph at the top of the syllabus that gives the instructor's overview of the course as carefully as they read the "terms of service" for their credit card, but it's worth a second glance. It will tell you how to write your paper, because it reveals what your instructor wants you to learn.

Instructors project an arc for the course through their syllabi, but their students, ideally, take it from there, molding a new course the instructor may not have imagined. The students you sit in a room with three hours a week will affect what you write about every bit as much as your instructor. Your class discussions should shape how you read any source you pick up for your paper. You may think your instructor is just waiting for someone to give that magical right answer, but they're not. While their students are talking, instructors are often thinking, "Dang that was smart. I have to include something about that on the syllabus next semester."

Listen closely to your fellow students, because the moment that tilts the whole class on its head could come from anywhere—the student who talks too much or the one in the back who rarely talks at all. It's great when a class is upended by one student's comment. Papers are born in such moments. For this reason, I encourage my students to cite their peers' comments in their papers.

Of course, when you do write your paper, your own unique paper, it will draw on sources that you alone have collected and read. But as you assemble those sources from the library and the Internet, remember: Every source for your paper is also an audience. Speak back to everything you read for your paper. Pick fights with all your sources—particularly the ones you agree with.

Also, with each source you read, think of someone else in your class who would benefit from what you found. My favorite thing about teaching is having students email me random crap they come across that relates to what we're reading right then. Your paper should give your instructor and your peers something to think about. Write your paper as if it should be added to your instructor's syllabus the following year under "Required Reading." It just might.

What Sources Are Allowed in a Research Paper?

When you're looking for sources, it pays to be choosy, because one bad source can rot your whole paper. When your instructor reads your paper, half of their evaluation of your effort will be formed when they look at your works cited page. Quality is key. A good paper does not have the most sources. It has the best sources.

How do you find the best sources for your paper? Do you thumb through the back issues of *People* at your dentist's office until you find some articles that look like what you're writing about? Not so much. Do you run a Google search and click on the first three links? Not if you want an A. Do you go to the library, find the shelf with roughly the right material, and start scanning titles? Well, that's how we used to do it, but that was before databases put refined search capability at our fingertips.

To write a good research paper, you have to be a tireless and savvy searcher. Serendipitous discovery as a research process is overrated. The percentage of academics who "stumble" onto a great find is misrepresented in modern movies, where everyone seems to pick up the right book just at the moment they need it. Real academics don't "stumble" onto their best discoveries. We stumble over to our nearest librarian the moment we feel ourselves stumble at all.

I can't give you a foolproof series of steps for finding the right sources for your paper, but I can give you these tried and true guidelines:

First, look at the assignment to find out what kind of sources you should use.

There are different kinds of sources: Secondary sources are sources written by other people about your topic. Primary sources are witnesses to history—artifacts, interviews you collect, materials you find in the world or in the archives.

On your assignment sheet, your instructor may tell you what sources are acceptable. Does your instructor want you to look for peer-reviewed academic articles or newspaper articles, or to draw from only the texts used in class? Do they want you to do primary research? If the assignment doesn't specify what sources are acceptable, ask your instructor.

Second, know what you're looking for before you search.

Every paper you write in college begins with you: your interests, your questions, your hunches. If you don't have at least some sense of what your paper is about before you search, you're not going to find answers in someone else's book. Make a list of what you need to find out before you start searching, and you'll maintain some sense of your own voice in the paper. Go out clueless, and you might wind up presenting your instructor with a disconnected pile of quotes.

Third, look in the right place.

You can't find bread in a hardware store. And you won't find academic journal articles in a library database that covers only newspapers. Make sure you're searching in the right place for the sources you need.

Fourth, just because you read it doesn't mean you should use it.

This seems obvious, but it's easily forgotten once you get into the details of writing the paper. If the book you found doesn't help you answer your question, toss it. If your question is about why the campus dining hall went trayless, for example, you can't find that out by asking students, even if students are standing all around you. They don't know. Get an interview with an administrator in dining services.

Some sources are just bad.

Sure it depends on your purpose, but no one really wants to see a quotation from *People* in an academic paper. You need to go where the story is. The story is never in *People*.

Why Do We Read Each Other's Drafts?

If you're in a college writing class, chances are you'll be asked to read and respond to the writing of your peers, and give your own work to peers for comment. Writing groups and peer review, you might think, are shadowy devices to get your fellow students to do the work the instructor should be doing. Why should you be showing your work to your classmates? What do they know? The answer is, insofar as your paper is concerned, almost everything. The reader, like the customer, is always right.

A lot of writers wind up waiting tables and learn this the hard way. I'm no exception. In the summer between my junior and senior years in college I worked in a Friendly's chain restaurant in the Catskill Mountains of New York State. By night, I was a tie–dye–wearing, Grateful Dead–following, patchouli–soaked hippie; by day, I wore white nurse's shoes, panty hose, and a blue and white houndstooth uniform with an apron. This outfit was capped off with a nametag proclaiming, "I'm Cathy, and I'm Friendly."

Friendly I was not. And neither were the customers. Most of the patrons of this ice cream–heavy establishment were in middle school. Some of them would leave tips under inverted full glasses of water. Others wouldn't leave any tip at all. I had great difficulty mustering the requisite cheer to live up to my nametag. Even my boyfriend, the one time he ate lunch at the restaurant, suggested I smile more.

There is a story that once when a customer asked me if the soup I was about to serve him was warm, I stuck my finger in it and said "yes." I don't remember this.

My mother, who made periodic surprise trips upstate to make sure I wasn't on drugs, was so alarmed by my bitchiness and death–like pallor that she sent me to get a blood test. Turned out I had mononucleosis. I also was poor and needed the job, so I kept working. Bad news for anyone who ordered the soup.

Perhaps some of you have been servers, and thus good tippers for the rest of your lives. If you were, you may remember a sign much like the one Friendly's had in the staff break room: a flowery, possibly cross–stitched number with the motto, "The customer is always right."

We servers would probably rewrite this as "The grill is always slow," but the point is not about where blame *really* lies. It's a statement about a relationship. You can't be right if you're the server, because your job is to make the customer happy, which you can't do if you're arguing with them.

For the same reason, the bass player is always right in a band (because they're the root of the chord), and the man is always right when you waltz (because the man always leads;

I hate waltzing). In all these relationships, someone gets to determine what action counts, and everyone else has to suck it up.

I now adopt something like this "customer" motto when I teach students how to listen to feedback from their peers. I tell them about Friendly's, the nametag, the daily humiliation, the passive–aggressive payback with the soup. And then I tell them that just like the customer, the reader is always right. Believing this is absolutely crucial to receiving feedback and benefiting from it.

The person reading your paper is right. They are also smarter than you, or so you need to believe for the amount of time they are giving you feedback. You have everything in the world to learn from them. If they say a paragraph is confusing, they're right. If they say there's a leap in logic, they're right. If they say that cute anecdote you worked so hard on for your introduction doesn't work—yes, even if it contains the best sentence of all time, *of all time*—they're right. You need to stand there, just like a server, and take it. And then ask them if they would like fries with that.

Even the least experienced writer can turn out to be the keenest detective when finding flaws in the drafts of others. That kid with the camouflage backpack may not say the smartest things in class, but he'll be right that something is wrong with your paper. As long as peers stay away from trying to correct your grammar (you need their help on your argument, not on technical details), you're getting an advance look at what your instructor will mark later. You should tip your peer editor.

A caveat: While the reader is always right that there is a problem, they are often wrong when making suggestions about how to fix it. Readers can only remark on what's on the page, and what your paper needs may not be on the page yet.

When it comes to finding out what's not on the page yet, nothing beats a conversation. In a conversation, you as the writer can communicate what you really want to say, but didn't write, because you felt you couldn't—or shouldn't. You can reveal where you stopped talking to real readers and started talking just to teachers, where you sold your original goals down the river. You can listen to your peers, and then, when their orders are in, tell them your story of struggle. Let them help you find your way.

What Do I Say about Someone Else's Draft?

Your friend has handed you their paper and asked what you think. You feel nervous because you know that you have to find something to praise. All writers want you to love what they wrote. They want you to see their brilliance. That's a lot of pressure. So what do you say?

It's great. It flows. You have a strong thesis. These are the kinds of comments I hear when papers are passed around for peer review in college composition classes. Such comments are well meant, but they rarely make writers feel better about what they wrote. Writers can tell that such praise is empty. "You have a strong thesis" is the "Hi, how are you?" you throw out to people as you pass them on the sidewalk and don't even stop to listen to the answer. Such comments don't make papers any better, either.

Even worse is when this faint praise is just used to cushion the blow of criticism—the proverbial "praise sandwich." I've never understood the praise sandwich. Sandwiches are defined by what's on the inside, not by what's on the outside.

A PBJ on rye or white is still a PBJ. Even if you wrap nasty comments in the nicest praise, you're still serving up a dirt sandwich.

So what should you do about praise? A former mentor of mine, Chet, used to say, "You can always find something specific to praise in someone else's paper." I tested this credo when he attended a presentation I gave just days after I'd been told my father was dying of lung cancer. In a fog I stepped up to the podium and mumbled for my allotted fifteen minutes. After it was over, Chet came up from the audience and, nearly stuttering, managed to eke out, "Well, you stuck to the time limit!"

I didn't think it possible for me to feel worse, but Chet's comment put the coffin nail in my already weak will to live that day. Knowing that he had been straining through the whole second half of the presentation for something specific to praise, and that praising the fact that my paper wasn't any longer was the best he could do. I just hugged him and sobbed.

Best not to worry about what to praise or criticize in someone else's work. Just listen to what the paper is saying. Then restate the argument in one sentence. This trick works even better if several people read the paper at once and give their own one–sentence summary. Then, you can all fight like cats over who is right.

Maybe you've read the paper three times, and you still can't figure out what it's trying to say. You can't even get a pulse. Just give the writer a brilliant idea that you're not using. It's allowed, and it is, unlike faint praise, truly generous. It's not like you're writing the paper for them. If they really are undeserving, they won't be able to make anything out of it anyway.

If you want to help another writer, whether you're in peer review or in your dorm room editing for your best friend, don't think first about what you can say that will make them happy. Don't think about meeting your quota of criticism either. In fact, just forget about evaluating altogether, either thumbs up or thumbs down. Remind yourself that this writer already has a teacher. You don't have to say the "right" thing. Just say your thing.

When Should I Quote and When Should I Paraphrase?

I once asked how many of my students had skipped reading a big, chunky quote in the middle of our textbook. Every hand went up, including my own. I've trained myself not to read big quotes. You probably have, too, because you know that the author is going to summarize that quote in one sentence right after it appears. Right?

So why even include those quotes?

It's been liberating for me to realize I don't have to. If I can paraphrase a big quote in one sentence (and cite the source, of course), I delete the quote entirely.

This insight I credit to my writing partner, Nancy Abelmann, a brilliant anthropologist who has zero patience for big quotes. Nancy and I show each other almost everything we write before we show it to anyone else. As readers, we tell each other what we think. What we really think. To give each other permission to rip a draft to shreds, we write on the top of it: "I have no ego."

Once, she wrote over a sentence of mine I loved, "I'm a smart person and I don't understand this so take it out." Just like that. Several steps ahead of me, she had already figured out that even after one hundred revisions, that sentence wouldn't make my writing better.

Another time, halfway through reading a big, chunky quote I'd slapped in the middle of a page, she turned to me and asked, "Do I really need to read this?"

I had not yet reached the stage with Nancy where I sat like a server taking orders as she went up and down my draft. I did my best to justify the quote's existence. She was unmoved. On her fourth book and third kid, she had no time to waste. She explained her bar for quoting instead of paraphrasing—something that has been my guide ever since: "If you're not going to use this quote to make at least two points, just paraphrase it. Use every quote two ways."

A quote should serve multiple functions in your paper. Does it support your argument? Great! But that shouldn't be the only thing it does. It could support a claim that you're making, at the same time as it opens up a new problem for your paper to work through. Does the quote present a counter–argument to your thesis? Fine. But, again, that shouldn't be the only thing it does. It could serve as a point of debate, and at the same time identify the audience that your paper addresses, or the limits of your claims, or the scope of the problem you address.

How do you get a quote to do two things? Read it more than once. Challenge yourself to come up with not two, but three, four, or five observations you could make about that quote. I think of every quote as a lemon, and I'm trying to make a pitcher of lemonade. I give it a good twist, then another, then another. I need every drop I can get out of it.

I realize that the undying allure of the big, chunky quote is that it makes your paper longer. Running half a page short with only an hour to go until submission time? Why not add a big, chunky quote? After all, there's no limit on the amount of characters the cut–and–paste function can teleport into your draft.

Sadly, quotes added for the purpose of making a paper seem longer only make a paper worse. Think of word count in terms of quality, not quantity: words that don't contribute to your argument don't help your paper. For a college paper, your challenge is not simply to write the required number of words, but to make a compelling argument.

Mentally, put my friend Nancy on your shoulder as you write. She'll ask, "Do I really need to read this?" Make sure you can answer, "Yes."

 ## Can I Use "I"?

The short answer: Yes. But please, keep reading.

"Can I use 'I' in my paper?" is probably the number–one question I hear students ask their college composition instructors. And the response they receive is always a version of the one I've given above: Yes.

Yes, you can refer to yourself as "I" to demonstrate your authorship of your college paper. The first–year composition classroom that would tell you "no" is not one I would want to be in. A "no" would have to ignore overwhelming evidence that published academic writers use "I" constantly. They do so to explain their methods, acknowledge their prejudices, and identify their arguments as theirs.

And because writing without using "I" is a pain in the ass.

If you choose to eliminate one of the most frequently employed words in the English language, you've just made your paper ten times harder to write. You've limited your options, because in many situations, "I" is the most accurate word to use.

Without "I," you'll have to write things like "the author believes" or "it has been observed" or "one can see." These phrases aren't just stuffy. They're vague. Who is the "one" in "one can see"? Can every "one" see equally well? Usually, no.

Of all the substitutions for "I," the most dangerous is "we." Using "we" instead of "I" means that you are speaking for others you allege share a viewpoint or experience. The only people who get to use "we" instead of "I" are pregnant women and the Queen of England. If you're writing your paper with others, and those others are

also named as authors, then sure, use "we." But, more often than not, an instructor will be quick to note if they have been enrolled in a "we" against their will.

Ultimately, using "I" or avoiding "I" won't make much difference in your grade. College writing isn't about sticking to a list of dos and don'ts. If it were, a year of composition could be boiled down to a four–hour walkthrough of warnings and consequences—something like a driver safety course for speeders.

Your paper will not be evaluated on whether or not you use "I," but rather on how you use "I."

Ask yourself: What is your "I" saying? Who does your "I" think they are? Is your "I" someone searching for the answer to a significant question, or someone who just wants to voice an unsupported opinion? That second "I" is not going to do so well.

In sum, you can—and should—use "I" in your paper, because avoiding it will make you miserable and your paper worse. Without "I," you'll have difficulty clearly distinguishing your thoughts from those of others you are citing (and making such distinctions is one of the functions of academic writing). Without "I," you'll struggle to own your observations as distinct from general statements of fact. Without "I," you may forget that this paper is yours and that you stand behind it. That reason to use "I" is the best one of all.

How Do I Get Over Writer's Block?

I'm a hopeless hypochondriac, and although I struggle with writing and sometimes despair, I know my problem is never writer's block. You don't have writer's block, either. Argue for writer's block and it's yours. But know, know that there are tools in your reach to get you writing again, and you'll be fine.

First, a disclaimer (in the style of those commercials for Big Pharma's newest product): If you can't write even one word, treat that as a sign that you might have other issues needing attention and seek help for your distress first.

But if you are just having trouble focusing on a paper, you don't have writer's block. You're just stuck. When it comes to college writing, there are two main reasons for getting stuck.

(a) You haven't done your research.

Your assignment probably requires that you say something in relationship to other texts, and to do that, you have to first locate and read those texts. You don't need inspiration. You need information—the right information—to complete the assignment. Find your sources, and if they're not the right sources, find others. Read them, read them again, and take lots of notes before turning back to the page. You'll be cranking away in no time.

Suppose, though, you've read all your sources and now you're midway through a paper, feeling you're still going nowhere. In that case, (a) is not your problem. Your problem is:

(b) You have what I'll call "writer's cramp."

Writer's cramp is similar to leg cramp, though it causes psychic rather than physical anguish. Check if you have any of the following symptoms:

- Rewriting the same sentence five times
- Logging on to Facebook
- Playing with the margins
- Flipping through the thesaurus
- HUGE, chunky quotes
- Rereading it and deciding it's great
- Rereading it and deciding it's crap

If you're experiencing writer's cramp, just stop even trying to write. Not forever, but for a little while. Writing is an athletic event. You could try to push through writer's cramp, just as you could keep running with a leg cramp, but it's not the best way to go for long-term health.

The brain is much like the leg—that is, it's a piece of your body. Brains and legs need the same things—fluids, carbs, protein, rest—in order to work optimally and eventually in order to work at all. Your brain, however, unlike your leg, has lots of things it's trying to do (including controlling your leg), which is why a full 20 percent of your heart's blood flow goes straight to it. Given the brain's workload, it can cramp not only because of low blood sugar and lack of sleep, but because of its inability to escape that recent fight with Mom/Dad/significant other, or that nagging thought that everyone in the world is at a party while you're trying to write this paper.

You know what? Call your parent or significant other and patch things up. Or just go to that party. You aren't getting anywhere anyway. Despite all you've heard, brains do not multitask well. Might as well enjoy your years in college.

And when you come back to the paper, sit down and think with your clearer mind: What am I missing? If you still can't see it, send your draft to a writing buddy in your class, or make an appointment with your university's writing tutorial center (because you've left yourself ample time for this contingency) and ask them to help you figure out what your paper needs.

The kind of patience needed to work out writer's cramp stems from a form of compassion. Cramp is your friend. It can tell you when to take a break, to step away from the computer, to stop pushing an argument that simply isn't working. It can remind you to stop pushing yourself past your limits, and most crucially, to ask for help when you need it.

By the way, composition instructors get what I'll call "grading cramp." Symptoms are too numerous to report but include counting the number of papers they have left to grade, over and over and over again. A side effect is crabby comments. It helps to have some compassion for the instructor, even if you were the one who got that comment

the instructor wrote while they were wearing their crabby–
pants. They should have just gone to that party.

Should I Quote the Dictionary?

No need to quote the dictionary. But you might consider adding to it.

Sometimes when you're searching for the right word for your paper, you can't find it in the dictionary. It's not in the thesaurus, either—not yet, anyway. It's the word you have to invent to describe what you're talking about. If you can make this word and make it right, you have your paper just where you want it.

The best writing intentionally (key word "intentionally") stretches language. Words come and go because language is alive, bowing to the whims of those who speak it. As a writer, you can take advantage of this fact by keeping your language fresh. You should, of course, avoid clichés (I'll repeat here the truism that a cliché is anything you've heard before, even once), but you can have a lot more fun with language than you think, even in college writing.

Consider the book *Freakonomics*, whose title combines the words "freak" and "economics" to make an entirely new "word." A book about economic theory's potential to explain a range of social phenomena doesn't sound like something that would fly off the shelves. And yet to date, *Freakonomics* has sold millions of copies worldwide and spawned several sequels, a *New York Times* column, a podcast, and a movie. The title worked. It turned heads and was easy to remember. Just as crucially, it encapsulated the book's argument that economic theory could explain freak happenings, such as why drug dealers live with their mothers.

How about a new phrase? In a congressional hearing, entomologist May Berenbaum dubbed honeybees "six-legged livestock" to explain that pollinators are just as crucial to our food chain as cows and pigs. Just like that, she made her cause memorable and supportable. No legislator wants to be labeled an environmentalist wacko for passing laws to protect an insect; safeguarding the nation's livestock, however, makes Beltway bureaucrats look like cowboys. In a good way.

You might be thinking: I'm not writing a best-selling book, nor am I testifying before Congress. I'm only trying to get through my college writing course. I can't coin new words there.

Try anyway. Attempting to work out a brand–new word will force you to think about all words more. If your instructor has questioned your word choice, spend more time with the dictionary. Think about where and how words get their meaning. And how people use them, or no longer use them, for their own purposes.

Then try making a new word for the central insight of your paper. A caution here: Your word has to make sense. There's a chasm of difference between Berenbaum's "six–legged livestock" and "bihog," the "word" I attempted in a Scrabble game when I was eleven. (Under my family's scorching glare, I failed to provide a plausible definition for "bihog" and was banished from the game.) Your word should appear in quotation marks at least the first time you use it. Quotation marks show your awareness that either you've created a word, or you're using an established word in a non–standard way.

The payoffs are immense should you be successful in your efforts to coin a word or figure of speech. Most English instructors can't resist evidence that their students are aware of language and what can be done with it. It's one of their weaknesses. When English professors go out to a music club, they don't listen to the band. They're too busy talking. Language, to them, is simply the most entertaining, beautiful, creative thing in the world. They became English instructors because they fell in love with books that did something with language they had never seen done before; they reserve the greatest scorn for books filled with what has been said, and said again.

If you think experimenting with language in your composition class is too great a risk, look at it this way: You're much more likely to irritate your instructors by using a word the dictionary finds acceptable, but they don't, such as "monetize," "utilization," or "impact" (as a verb). The dictionary is nothing but a canvas. And we are all language's painters.

How Do I Write a Strong Thesis Statement?

There is only one way to write a strong thesis: Write a strong paper.

Strong words in a thesis do not make it strong. A thesis that is controversial is not necessarily strong. No one can tell you your thesis is strong just by reading it unless they have read the rest of your paper because no thesis is inherently "strong."

An example:

> The expansion of nuclear power in the United States would solve our energy crisis.

Is that a strong statement? Yes. It makes a controversial assertion. It takes a stand. It looks into the future and does not blink. However, is it a strong thesis statement? I have no idea. If the rest of the paper can convince me that it is accurate with some hard evidence, then it is a strong thesis statement.

If the paper can't make the case, however, that thesis is just an unsupported claim. A thesis is effective only when supported by the evidence and arguments presented in the rest of the essay. A strong statement presented as a thesis with no evidence to back it up is like a Trojan Horse with no Trojans in it: all show and no follow–through. It's a towering oak with no roots. One stiff wind and it's over.

Don't get too attached to a thesis statement early in your project. Your research will change your argument—and it should. As you write, remember that a thesis is there to be tested not just by others, but also by you. The word "essay" comes from the French meaning "to try." Your thesis statement is always on trial. It's your client. Like a good lawyer, you want to prep a convincing case to defend that client. But, unlike a good lawyer, you should throw in the towel the moment you perceive serious cracks.

Although you can't identify a strong thesis without reading the entire paper, you can pick out a weak one in two seconds. A weak thesis includes a vague term or makes a statement so generic that it cannot be disproved.

An example:

Malcolm X was a product of his times.

Arguing for the influence of "the times" on any person, place, or thing is tempting because it's always true. Budget deficit? A product of its times. Helicopter parenting? Impossible without technology, so a product of its times. Disco music, cilantro in everything, the mullet? All easily dated products of their times.

Just because a statement is true doesn't mean it needs to be said in an academic paper. One tip for avoiding the generic thesis: If you can substitute any person, place, or thing as the subject of your thesis statement, and that statement would still be true, you have a weak thesis.

The thesis hobbled by vagueness is a common response to the ill–advised "compare and contrast" paper assignment.

An example:

> The 1996 movie *Romeo and Juliet* is similar to
> the original play because both are dramatic,
> but they tell their story in different ways.

The words "similar" and "different" are capable of establishing a relationship between any two things in the universe. Brad Pitt and I are similar. We're both made of molecules. But come to think of it, we both share that attribute with the chair I'm sitting on. Even when the similarity or difference is specified (we are similarly made of molecules, but different in that only one of us has millions of dollars), we're still left with the huge "who cares" question. Why is it significant that Brad Pitt and I are both made of molecules? Who would not expect differences between a play and a movie?

Make your life easier. Don't use the words "similar" or "different" in your thesis (even if the assignment seems to invite you to).

In general, think more about what your thesis does for your reader. The thesis is the line that sets your reader's expectations for the rest of the paper. It is a promise. With your thesis you tell the reader: Here is what I will try to prove.

You don't want to break that promise, so consider as you craft your thesis what your evidence will allow you to say. Break that promise, and you break your relationship to the reader. Maintaining the strength of that relationship, not the strength of your thesis, is what writing is all about.

✒ How Do I Write an Introduction?

You may have heard your introduction should start with the general and move to the specific. In reality, the best introductions start with the specific. After that, they get even more specific.

Just how specific? Imagine, for a moment, that you have heart failure, and that you will die in a matter of days unless surgery to replace a faulty valve in your aorta succeeds. Your surgeon has just come into your room to explain the procedure. How would you want your surgeon to start this explanation? With a description of heart surgery techniques throughout the ages? With a chipper  anecdote about the first time they saw a real human heart in medical school and almost puked? How about a line from a

Shakespeare sonnet about the heart? Most likely, you would want your surgeon to explain what they're going to do when they take a knife to your heart.

My uncle was in just this situation. After going into heart failure some years ago in his house in rural New Hampshire, he was flown to a top-drawer Boston hospital to be prepped for open-heart surgery. Right before the operation, the cardiac surgeon appeared at his bed to tell him what they were going to do: saw through the breastbone, shut down the heart, fix that valve. If they couldn't fix it, they would insert a valve from a pig. Did my uncle consent?

Surgeons are not known for their people skills. They probably became surgeons to avoid the discomfort of having to deal with people who are awake. My uncle's surgeon did not waste time trying to either terrify or console. "He got straight to the point and kept going," my uncle reported with a smile from his recovery room. This is the kind of man you want delivering news to you on how you're going to stay alive.

People mistakenly think that writing is like bowling, that to get the ball rolling you have to start with a big windup from the beginning. The very beginning. Taken to an extreme, this approach yields something like this:

> Since the dawn of time, college students in first–year composition classes everywhere in the universe have begun their papers following a hallowed tradition. Who knows where this tradition came from? We only know that even here, in the United States, students today still follow that tradition. They begin their papers with the most general statement possible, proceed to a rhetorical question that cannot be answered, and then offer up another statement with which few could disagree before getting to the task at hand: articulating the subject of the paper you are now reading, which follows in the tradition long established.

It's easy to point out what is wrong with this introduction. Colleges haven't been around since the dawn of time. And when exactly is the "dawn of time" anyway? Can I get a citation for that?

I have never read an introduction that used the apocryphal "dawn of time" phrase, but I have read sprawling introductions that narrate most of the history of gene therapy, or skiing, or Internet dating. Even if it's the history of something as brief as your lunch, it's probably more background than your readers need.

People write long and winding introductions because they're writing their way to what they want to say. The problem is that readers don't read the way writers write; readers want to get to the point. Their clock is ticking. Maybe they're not going to die in a matter of hours, but they do have lots of things vying for their attention besides your paper—the papers of the other twenty students in the class, for example, if your reader is your instructor. Remember, there's plenty of room later in your paper for any necessary backstory. It doesn't all need to go up front, where your main point should be.

When you sit down to write, imagine that you're no longer a student. You're a cardiac surgeon at one of the top hospitals in the nation facing the patient you'll be cutting into in the morning. Put on your scrubs. Make your rounds. Skip the small talk. Get straight to the point and keep going.

How Can I Make My Paper Flow?

If you're worried about your paper's flow, take another look at the assignment your instructor gave you. I would bet my iPhone that nowhere in that grading rubric does it say, "Flow: 30%."

I have never had an experienced writer hand me a piece of their writing and ask if it flows. So lately I've started to wonder, what is flow, really? How did flow become that thing instructors never ask for, but students feel they have to provide?

When I ask my students to tell me what flow is, the definitions they come up with suggest smooth, unbroken writing, a stream of effortless words. You never see the writer work. You never pause to question. You are pulled from one paragraph to the next by a master conductor, an entertaining traffic cop, or the Force—someone, or something, that makes every word seem inevitable.

We would all like our readers to become so absorbed in our work that they don't put it down, skip ahead, or spend time considering what they'd rather be reading. But experienced writers know that to achieve that, they have to stop thinking about the words in front of them, and start thinking about the people who will be reading those words.

They have to imagine a very particular reader, with very particular quirks, habits, and biases, and then wonder:

- What does this reader already know?
- What will this reader expect me to know?
- What questions will this reader have that I can anticipate?
- What opinions might this reader hold that I can address?
- How can I introduce new information in a way they will understand?
- How can I take this reader from their familiar to my familiar?
- What do I want this reader to remember?

Experienced writers know that if they can't answer these questions, they will be unable to create the experience of untroubled reading. They know that peppering their paper with transitional phrases, such as "however," "additionally," "another," "therefore," or even "with regard to," will get them nowhere. Why? Suppose I told you, "I eat a quart of ice cream every night. Therefore, I stay skinny."

You may have heard that you can't polish a turd. And you can't cover up an argument that doesn't make sense with a transitional phrase. A paper with glaring leaps of logic will cause your reader to pause, irrespective of however many "howevers" are in there.

At the end of the day, experienced writers think less about an abstract quality the ideal paper should have, and more about what their very real readers expect. And what those readers expect can only be poorly approximated by the notion of "flow."

Plenty of great academic writing is ridden with disjuncture: subheadings, sections, and other breaks that signal at least a partial change of focus. If the reader expects those subheadings, no harm, no foul. Flow is in the eye of the beholder.

If your peer tells you, "I think it was great. It seemed to flow," then press harder. The truth is, most people are polite; they're not sure they're allowed to remark on anything except whether or not a paper "flows." If you want to write a good paper, let them know that you're different. Tell them: "I don't care whether it flows or not. Tell me what I said." When they give their answer, you'll have all you need to know.

How Do I Outline My Paper?

The traditional outline is a skeletal organization of the paper you plan to write.

There's an old expression: If you want to see God laugh, talk about your plans. If your outline falls apart somewhere in the middle of writing, don't beat yourself up. The best papers are full of twists and turns that are hard to see in advance. Much like a vacation that didn't go as planned, but left you with much better stories.

For this reason, rather than outlining your paper before you start, I suggest writing a reverse outline of your first draft.

For a reverse outline, treat your first draft as though you are the reader. Take notes on each paragraph in the margin: What does each paragraph tell you? How does it take you from one idea to the next? You might write something like, "This paragraph tells the reader why my research is important." Or, "This paragraph explains to the reader what previous scholars have said about my research." Or, "This paragraph answers the reader's counter–argument."

Then, look at your marginal notations. Every paragraph should do something different.

If you've made two similar notations, you're probably making the same point in different words.

If you can't explain how your note on one paragraph relates to your note on the next one, you've probably made a conceptual leap that is not yet grounded in evidence.

Once you've discovered where your argument stalls, how do you fix it? Step back from your draft, turn the computer off (or flip the paper over), and go talk to someone—your instructor, a peer, someone outside the class—because what you need to fix your paper isn't on the page yet. Have a conversation about your work in progress with another potential reader to find out where you're stuck, and where to go from there. They'll help you figure out what's missing. And it will be the kind of thing you never thought you'd need to say when you began.

You can tell yourself a lot of lies about what your paper will do by writing a traditional outline, but a reverse outline tells you what you actually did. Give it a try.

How Can I Make My Paper Stand Out from the Pile?

A paper that stands out is one that tackles an important problem.

I once asked students to write about what bothered them about their university. What makes you mad? I asked. What would you most like to change? I got one essay on the university budget (collapsing), one on the lack of professors in introductory classes, another on corruption in the admissions process, three on icky dining–hall food, and five on the bus system and its failure to adhere to its announced schedule.

The university budgets, the disappearance of the professoriate from undergraduate classes, and the admissions process had all drawn national attention that year. The essays on dorm food cited weight–related illnesses as a concern—also national news.

The bus essays, however, struggled to articulate the significance of the problem of late busses. In this struggle, the effect of late busses was inflated to create an insupportable claim: People are literally freezing while waiting for the bus.

Imagine, for a minute, a smug Norwegian reading one of the bus essays. Smug Norwegians will tell you that there's no such thing as bad weather, just bad clothes.

For our next class, on a sixteen–degree day, I walked the twenty minutes from my house to our classroom wearing five layers, including my hideous Gore–Tex, seam–sealed, rated–to–thirty–degrees–below–zero parka. Sweating profusely, parka Velcro–ed to my eyeballs, I asked my students if any of them would leave their dorm room dressed like me to wait for the bus. They were so sweet. They looked at me with pity—some with alarm. They agreed that the parka would keep them warm, though they also told me that it'd be hard to be seen in public wearing it.

That day we also noticed that 25 percent of the women in the class—four out of sixteen—were wearing the identical black fleece jacket. It costs more than my parka, offers poor wind protection, but is super–cute. We then discussed whether people freeze because of late busses, bad weather, or peer pressure to underdress.

A real problem interests a diverse readership. I had one African American student in my class that semester. He did not wear premium–brand clothing. A twenty–four–year–old, married, non–traditional student, a veteran of the war in Iraq, he was perplexed by why students didn't just run between classes to stay warm, but felt he couldn't say so in class (he stayed around afterward to disclose this). He was floundering on the essay for utterly different reasons than his classmates; compared to his time in the Iraq, he wrote, nothing seemed like a problem to him anymore. Even if he had wanted to conform to his surroundings at a college where he, as an African American student, represented a dwindling single–digit percentage of the undergraduate population, he would have known that wearing the "in" jacket wouldn't help him blend in.

Here are some real problems that might have interested him:

- The escalating cost of public higher education

- The rapidly dwindling population of African American students on major public university campuses
- The difficulties involved in transitioning from military to civilian life

Any one of these problems would have to be whittled down to manageable size before it could be treated in an academic paper. A paper that addressed the escalating cost of a public higher education, for example, could focus on one contributing factor, whether declining state support, university–level management of existing funds, or dwindling sources of financial aid. But before that paper could convince multiple audiences, they would need to be imagined—the African American vet, the smug Norwegian—audiences both in the class and beyond it.

To think about what problems interest a diverse readership, picture your essay plastered on the departure board of an international airport. Imagine people strolling past to read it. What would they say if they could leave an anonymous comment? How could you convince them that your problem was worth their time?

How Do I Avoid Being Caught Plagiarizing?

I sympathize with students who feel the urge to plagiarize. It can seem an absurd task to come up with something original to say about a topic you've only been asked to think about for a month. I have a lot of sympathy with any writer, experienced or not, who has to grasp for words that don't feel like their own, and use them as if they were. Who wouldn't look around for models?

With the Internet, plagiarizing is much easier than it used to be. But the Internet cuts both ways. Catching plagiarism is also much easier than it used to be. So tempting as it may be, just don't do it.

These days your F for plagiarizing is just a Google click away—or not even that far. Most instructors can tell a bought paper just by reading it. How? The same way a dermatologist can tell a cancerous mole from one that looks a little weird but really is nothing: They've seen a million of them.

I used to know professors who lived to bust plagiarizing students. When a suspicious paper crossed their desk, it made their day. No longer a writing instructor, they became Sherlock Holmes. They'd comb the stacks of the library, looking for that one book from which the student had copped a sentence. At the bar with colleagues after class they'd trade stories of their greatest busts: "Last week I caught a student who plagiarized my own book, can you believe it?" Chortle, chortle, pip, pip, clink glasses.

Those days are over. The war between professors and students has gone cyber: Students lift material from online sources, and professors, using sophisticated software programs paid for by their universities, go online and bust them. Technology has taken all the fun out of plagiarism detection. No more thrill of the hunt.

Personally, I never understood the allure of busting students. I would rather spend my time teaching those who want to learn than busting those who don't. When I get a paper I know has been plagiarized, I just require the student to rewrite it over and over until it's better than the one they bought. You learn as much trying to fix a bad paper as you do writing your own. You can learn a lot about what makes a good paper from understanding why plagiarized papers are always bad. They all fail to do what a good paper must: Respond to the context of the class.

How do I know when a paper has been bought? It doesn't address any of the issues presented in class up to that point. It doesn't speak the class's language. It doesn't understand the class's sense of humor (and all classes should develop a particular sense of humor throughout the term). Whether fluently or not, it speaks another language. It makes no reference to current events, even where such a reference might be appropriate. It seems out of time and out of place, as if it had parachuted in from above.

And sometimes, if it's been cut and pasted from another Word document, I can just view the properties of the file to see who originally wrote it.

A good paper, on the other hand, talks back to the class. It acknowledges the preoccupations of classmates. It enters an ongoing conversation, engaging at least some of the terms of that conversation. Any paper that fails to enter that conversation is a bad paper, whether plagiarized or not.

I also know that if a class fails to provide students with an opportunity to enter a conversation, it invites a plagiarized paper. If a class offers students stock topics and no opportunity to contribute their knowledge or concerns, it practically begs for a quick fix from an online paper mill. Unfortunately, students are too often treated as potentially illicit consumers of knowledge, rather than as producers of knowledge. Talk to your instructor if you feel tempted to plagiarize. Tell them you want to do well but you're struggling. Make a genuine effort, and I promise you'll be better off in the long run.

I Keep Getting B's on My Papers. How Do I Get an A?

Let's say you're in the middle of writing your paper when you find a piece of information that simply does not fit, one that weakens the argument you were working to build. Your first impulse might be to delete this outlier from your draft. Don't. You have just found the game changer, which, if handled successfully, will turn your B paper into an A paper.

To understand the power of the game changer, imagine the following scenario: Your best friend has phoned to tell you about the new love of her life. He's handsome, he's rich, he sends her flowers, remembers her birthday, makes her laugh, and listens to her when she's had a tough day.

There's just one other thing about him—she wasn't going to mention it because she doesn't want to seem picky, because it is just one little thing, and really doesn't have anything to do with their relationship, so she should probably stay out of it, but, here goes—he cooks up methamphetamine in his basement.

Are you going to say, well, that's six positives and one negative, so go for it? No! The meth changes everything! The meth changes everything!

Not all discoveries are equal. Some discoveries are game changers. The meth is that point that doesn't seem to fit— and yet it does, oh yes it does. We now know why the boyfriend has lots of cash, for example. We also know why, despite all the hedging, she has told you about it; she can't ignore it any longer. She had to work herself up to confess, of course, so she saved this most important piece of information for the end.

Forget your friend for a minute, and return to your paper. Look again at that piece of evidence, that observation, that fact that doesn't fit with the rest of what you've written. It spoiled the story you were telling, so you don't like it. If you're wondering why you can't just delete it, however, consider your best friend's dilemma: Imagine that instead of taking your very sound advice—run like hell—she decides to keep seeing the tweaker. You know what? The meth still changes everything. Try as she might to ignore this unsavory detail about her boyfriend, the knowledge that she will someday wake up to find a few of his teeth on the pillow next to her and her wallet gone will ruin every otherwise enjoyable moment. The truth cannot be edited away.

The inconvenient discovery we make while researching and writing won't go quietly either; it nags at us, eats at us, until we deal with it. Granted, dealing with the game changer complicates life, revision—wise. There you are, writing that neat little paper, just five hundred words and a half hour from the finish line, when that fact, that stupid fact that doesn't fit, announces itself. There it is. The meth. Right smack dab in the middle of your draft. But now that you've recognized it, rejoice. Your story was boring without it and, on some level, unconvincing. Boring and unconvincing composition papers are B papers.

Fear keeps us trapped in the boring story. We want life to be happy, smooth, to always get better. B college papers tend to enact this want: The past is full of problems, people used to suffer racism and indifference, hardship and deprivation, but now, thankfully, in modern life we've figured out all that. Too many TV news human interest segments have wheedled their way into our brains, each—no matter how dire the situation—ending on an up note, rendered with the meticulous enunciation of the seasoned anchor.

It's not that the true story is necessarily the unhappy one, but it is the more complicated one. You get the A for dealing with complications, not ignoring them.

If you want to use the game changer to best effect in your paper, find the point that ruins your argument and go after it. Turn this gnarly point from a liability into your new best friend (because, let's face it, your current one has issues). Flip the paper over, and start brainstorming a new argument, because the insight you need to write your paper around—the game changer—isn't quite there yet; it's waiting for you to screw up your courage and look it squarely in the eye.

How Do I Back Up My Argument with Sources?

"I need backup" is what cops on cop shows yell when they feel outgunned and want another body to double their show of force "through the door." You, too, may feel outgunned as you launch into your paper's argument. College writing asks you to speak "up" to an instructor who has the authority to decide whether or not your argument makes the grade. It seems logical that a quote from an academically validated expert supporting your position would multiply your argument's force.

An academic paper must cite authoritative sources in order to be credible. You gain your reader's trust by showing that you have done the work of locating and citing existing scholarship on the subject of your research. But none of what you're going to find is going to "back up" your argument.

Here's why: In academic writing, only novel contributions to the knowledge pool are valued. Your quote from an expert reveals that someone has already asked, and answered, the same question as you. What, the reader then wonders, is your contribution?

Using a quote from an expert just to "back up" your argument will slowly corrode your own faith in what you have to say. You will start to think that without that expert there to ventriloquize your argument, it's not worthy of attention. In short, the more you go for "backup," the more you shrink.

Believe it or not, the expert who counts most in your paper is you. You are the author, and therefore the authority. Time to start thinking of those published experts not as supports on which you can lean, but as authors you can engage on a level playing field.

How do you engage with them? Tell your reader how what you're saying is different from (though related to) what the published expert said. Then tell the reader why that difference matters.

How about "backing up" your argument with a statistic or similar numerical factoid instead of a quote from an expert?

Conventional wisdom would dictate that you need facts to support your argument, and numbers make the best facts because no one can argue with a number.

In the words of Mark Twain (or whoever Mark Twain borrowed from), "There are three kinds of lies: Lies, damned lies, and statistics."

Numbers plopped in the middle of your paper do not make it more convincing. Academic readers, generally a skeptical bunch, get even more skeptical when faced with a statistic. They want to know: Who created that statistic? Where was it published? Who paid for the research that resulted in that statistic? What was the motivation for the research? And, most important, does the statistic have any relevance to the subject of the paper?

If you collected the statistic yourself, your readers will have questions about your methods as well. Your paper needs to anticipate and answer such questions. What makes you credible is not the statistic itself, but what you have to say about the statistic—your evaluation of its worth.

Remain the expert in your paper. It's easy to let your sources take over and let yourself fall into the role of ventriloquist's dummy, particularly if you've been told that you can't use "I" in academic writing (you can), or if you think you have nothing new or interesting to say (you do), or if you think composition instructors don't care about what their students have to say (they do).

One tip for staying out of the ventriloquist's dummy role is to start every paragraph with your voice. Rather than put another person's name or quote at the beginning of each paragraph, begin with your point, your take, your words. The first sentence of every paragraph is precious real estate. Consider it the beachfront property of your paper. Your readers will look there for your voice to guide them through everything that follows. No one, and nothing, can take your place. There is no "backup." There is only you, your reader, and the world of damned lies you walk through together.

How Do I Make My Paper Longer?

You don't need to make your paper longer. You just need to make it better.

Perhaps you've written six pages, and the assignment asks for eight to ten. And you really have nothing left to say. Forget about the page length. It's not your biggest problem.

Nationwide, a staggering number of five–to–seven– and eight–to–ten–page papers are assigned every day. The requirements of these papers vary tremendously—not only by instructor, course, and type of university, but also based upon the particular writing skill the assignment has been designed to help students develop.

In other words, the page limit is probably the last thing the instructor considered when creating the assignment.

And yet that page limit is bewitching. It's tangible, definite—one of the few things about college writing that is. But the problem with worrying about a paper's length is that you begin to think of writing in terms of quantity, whereas your instructor is concerned first and foremost about quality.

And thinking too much about quantity can lead you to try to game the system. Instructors know absolutely every hack there is for making a paper appear to be longer than it actually is. They know what the big fonts are. They recognize the difference between 1–inch margins and 1.25–inch margins at a glance. They know double–space from double–space–and–a–half. More instructors are requesting specific word counts instead of specific page lengths to avoid having to deal with such hacks, and online submission allows for a paper's word count to be checked within seconds.

Have you tried...

☐ 13 point font
☑ 1.10" margins
☐ Using a wider font family (Georgia!)
☐ Triple spacing
☐ More lines in header
☑ More paragraph indents

Of course, you want to write something approximately as long as the instructor requested. The page limit gives you a rough estimate of what your instructor expects in terms of detail. But that's all it gives you, and nothing more. Just get it in the ballpark.

The fact is, paper length, like time, is relative. If you've written a great paper that addresses all the elements specified in the assignment, your instructor will hardly notice the length. If you've written a paper that fails to address the assignment, presents no discernible argument, or is poorly supported by research, your instructor's eyes will automatically drift away from the prose down to the number at the bottom of the page. They'll start counting the pages of your paper, because they'd like it to end soon.

Think about the last bad movie you saw. You texted through it, right? A good movie, on the other hand, breezes along. Whether over two hours or just under ninety minutes, a good movie leaves you wanting more. That's the feeling you want your instructor to have as they read your paper. You don't want them to want more simply because of a number on the bottom of the page. You want them to want more because they didn't want your paper to end.

Maybe you don't think your paper could thrill an instructor to the same degree as a movie with a multimillion–dollar budget. Maybe thousands of people wouldn't line up and pay ten dollars to read your paper, but almost all the instructors I know get more lasting pleasure from reading a student's great work than from watching any number of blockbuster movies. Truly.

So how do you a make a paper better, rather than just longer? Accept that this assignment has given you a brand–new task, different from your last one, even if it has the same page limit. Relish the fact that your words have meaning. Choose each one carefully and well. We are, all of us, more than a number.

"He or She" or "They"?

Here's a famous riddle: A man and his son are in a car accident. The man dies, but the son is taken to a nearby hospital for emergency surgery. The surgeon looks at the patient and says, "I can't operate. This is my son." How is this possible?

I'm hoping this riddle is no longer a riddle, but I'll admit the first time I heard it I was stumped. How could the boy's father be the surgeon if he died in the accident? The answer, of course, is that the surgeon is a woman.

At least subliminally, many of us still think some jobs are for women, and others are for men. Growing up, I wanted to be a writer, but I thought I'd have to get a sex-change operation because all writers were men. No one had ever told me so, but no one had ever given me a book written by a woman, either. As I grew up, I started reading witty, profound, and brilliant women writers—Virginia Woolf, Toni Morrison, Nora Ephron—and I began to think maybe I could write, too.

I confess, I love it when people read my writing and assume I'm a man. There are so many stereotypes: what topics women are interested in (men), what their argument style is (gentle), what the covers of their books should look like (pink). If I can thwart any of those assumptions, I feel I've done my bit for gender equity. Men may be from Mars and women from Venus, but we're all hanging out in that messy middle that is the planet Earth. Let's not put people in boxes.

Happily, academic writing has confronted the box that is the gender–inaccurate generic pronoun "he" and dumped it into the recycling bin. Today, if you use "he" to refer to a category of persons (like writers or flautists) who could be men or could be women, you can expect your instructor to let you know that there are gender–neutral alternatives you could be using instead.

But what about the awkwardness of gender–neutral language? All those "him or her" and "he or she" phrases? How will the reader cope with a "they" that refers back to a singular subject? Isn't it best to keep language simple?

In academic writing, simplicity takes a back seat to accuracy. It might be "simpler" to say, for example, "The rain in Spain falls on the plain." But if sometimes the rain falls elsewhere, we need to acknowledge that, hence "The rain in Spain falls mainly on the plain." That extra word satisfies the skeptical reader (maybe).

How do you go gender-neutral in your writing? Here are some traditional options:

He or She

A very common choice. In every place you would have written "he," you write "he or she" instead. The upside of "he or she" is that it's accurate. The downside is that you may have to write a lot of these phrases in a paragraph. To avoid the bulk, some writers try:

S/he

"S/he" is less bulky than "he or she," but some people don't like the slash, so they try:

Alternating He and She

With this option you write "he" as the gender–neutral pronoun in one paragraph, and "she" as the gender–neutral pronoun in another. So if you're writing a research report on the Iraq War, for example, in one paragraph, your generic soldier might be a "he," in the next paragraph a "she." This option works in most cases. But suppose you're writing about the Civil War and not the Iraq War. All the (official) soldiers 150 years ago were men, so you can't alternate with accuracy. So that brings us to my preferred gender–neutral pronoun:

They

Using "they" instead of "he" is often my go–to strategy to avoid gender–inaccurate usage, because it is perfectly acceptable and has been for centuries. The singular "they" (also referred to as the "epicene they") appears in Shakespeare and other such stodgy, respectable literature. (Though what, in the end, is more gender–bending than Shakespeare's plays?) Even the *Oxford English Dictionary* thinks "they" is just fine.

Any of these gender–neutral options is better than calling everyone "he." And by "better," I mean not only less likely to hurt your grade, but also less likely to limit your view of the world. If you have been clinging to gender–inaccurate language, you may find the switch to gender–neutral language uncomfortable. For a while you might trip up when writing your sentences. That's okay.

When my friend "Daniel" moved to the West Coast, shaved his legs, and became "Danielle," it took a few months before saying "Danielle" became second nature to me. But it did. The beauty of people is that they change. The beauty of language is that it changes right along with them.

How Do I Answer the "So What" Question?

Every paper has to earn its reader's attention by answering the "so what" question: "So what if what you say is true? Why does it matter?"

Even for experienced writers, that's a really hard question to answer. It's too easy to think of people who don't care. So I've created a hack for the "so what" question. Instead of looking for the "so what" of your paper, try asking "so where" instead. Where are the people who will care about your paper? "So where" better helps you identify specific locations with audiences who have a stake in what you have to say.

As an example of the importance of "where," I offer my in–laws, my toughest audience. Born on the eve of the Great Depression to blacksmiths and ice deliverers, my in–laws know that life can turn on a dime, and God help you if your neighbors don't like you when it does.

Conversations at their house revolve around local happenings: births, foreclosures, deaths—increasingly deaths. In their northern Wisconsin community of eight thousand, devoid of Starbucks and nail salons, they are less than half a degree of separation away from almost everyone. My father–in–law, long the town's only pharmacist, is trusted for his discretion. My mother–in–law, the church organist for funerals, was renowned before her retirement for her fidelity to her profession: She had a police scanner in her kitchen and kept one ear cocked for reports of accidental death, so she would never miss a gig.

When it snows twenty inches they are the first on their block to shovel their walk. Then they shovel their neighbor's walk.

Around my in–laws, I feel shiftless, lazy, spoiled, and interesting in all the wrong ways. How could I not? They love me, so they ask what I'm writing lately. As I prattle on about my latest work in progress, I am sure my father–in–law has turned down his hearing aid. His steady gaze— honed by decades of listening to people disclose the locations of embarrassing boils—betrays neither amusement, nor curiosity, nor displeasure. He is patient. He waits until I've told my story, and remains silent for a moment longer. Then he asks if I'd like more cheese curds.

I lost him at hello. My in–laws frustrate me, as I frustrate them, but they teach me a valuable lesson: When it comes to my own fascinations, not even my relatives can feign enthusiasm. And so now when I'm writing a draft, I give my work in progress the provisional title "Who Gives a Crap," because it reminds me to write the bridge between my interests and my audience.

Why think about "where"? Because people's beliefs, tastes, and interests can't help but be shaped by their circumstances. As much as we all embrace a set of universal values, including the desire to see our children prosper and the hunger to do something meaningful with our lives, we are all also products of our surroundings. If we weren't, the networks wouldn't be able to call most elections with only 30 percent of the votes reported.

Answering "so where" forces you to find your paper a home. Ask yourself: Where are the people who would be affected by the issue I'm writing about? Are they in cities? Small towns? College campuses? Army barracks? Homeless shelters? Where do they work? On Wall Street? In fields? At home?

Once you figure out where they are, ask yourself: Where are they not? Where can they not afford to travel? What borders hem them in? Where do they feel outnumbered, out of place, lonely?

After you've considered your paper's home, tell your reader, directly. Tell them that your paper addresses an issue that emerges in certain places, in certain situations, with certain people. And then investigate the bridge you're building between your interests and your audience. How far can it extend to include others who might want a voice in the conversation you've started?

If your bridge doesn't extend far enough, turn the "so where" question on yourself: How do your circumstances shape your concerns? What issues seem not to reach you? What do you consider someone else's problem?

The truth is, I didn't listen to my in-laws' accounts of daily goings-on in their community with any more attentiveness than they listened to my lectures. I should have listened more. If the last decade of war, recession, and foreclosure has taught me anything, it's that my in-laws were right: Nothing is guaranteed. Life does turn on a dime. Take care of those neighbors, for we are all neighbors now.

How Do I Edit My Paper?

Bad papers are tortured around great sentences. To improve a paper, we often have to let go of the sentence we love the most.

Letting go is not easy. The year after I graduated from college, my landlord conducted a surprise cleaning of the basement of my apartment house, throwing out a box that contained my life's work. Everything I had written—every paper, every piece of fiction, every copy of a play that had been performed—had been in that box. All had been composed on a typewriter, so what was on paper was all I had. Or had had.

Faced with this loss, I entered the first stage of grief: total flipping idiocy. I decided I would find my box.

I called the city landfill to ask what I thought was a reasonable question: How could I locate an item from that week's garbage collection? I pictured my box perched neatly on a categorized pile of trash, waiting for me. The manager of the dump gently suggested I not try to recover it.

Okay, I wouldn't find the box. I decided to write down everything I remembered of what I'd lost. I went to a coffeehouse with notebook in hand to reconstruct at least one scene of the play from memory. As I recalled some of my favorite sentences, I hesitated. They weren't as good as I remembered. In fact, I couldn't imagine what I had ever seen in them.

I had always thought my play had been ruined by the actor who came to the performance drunk and referred to other cast members by their real names on stage—but no. The problems were much, much deeper. As I wrote sentence after sentence I had loved, I realized I would never bring the whole play back, and that was a good thing.

The same was true of my college papers. If I had written a nice–sounding sentence I would be captivated by it, unable to see that it added nothing to my argument. That sentence was standing between me and a good paper.

The difference between striving for a good sentence and striving for a good paper is the difference between infatuation and love. Infatuation is what we think love is until we learn, usually painfully, that it isn't. Intense, fleeting, and based solely on the allure of surface features— good hair, excellent musical taste, a perfect golf swing— infatuation is capable of seizing all our attention and energy. Then there's love, which, we're told by poets and pastors, endures even when we have seen each other at our worst. Love goes on hospital visits, checks into rehab, overlooks non–health–threatening weight gain. Love isn't flashy, but it's there when your teeth no longer are.

In other words, it's okay to have a crush on your sentences, but don't commit to them. Date your sentences. Marry your paper.

What your paper needs, like your love life, is attention to the big picture. It is possible that you are not the same person you were when you started the paper. Your goals and priorities have evolved. You may have outgrown that sentence that worked so well in your first draft. Let it go.

Find the sentence you like most in your draft and ask yourself: What does it contribute to my argument? How does it help the reader to understand my point? What is that sentence really saying? Is it so good it can't be made better?

If the answers to those questions aren't positive, it's time to bid farewell. Have faith, even as you strike the delete key, that you will write an even better sentence, one that actually fits in your paper. The best is yet to come. You will love again. This time, it will last.

How Do I Use a Semicolon?

Want to know how to use a semicolon? When to use single or double quotes? RTFM, baby.

"RTFM" is an acronym that emerged during the early years of tech support. But it is also useful as an answer to all grammar questions: "Read The F%&#ing Manual."

Correct grammar is as simple as reading a grammar manual and following the rules as you write. Use the manual your instructor assigned, or, if your instructor didn't assign one, take ownership of your usage and buy one yourself. Asking your college instructor to devote hours to explaining well–

documented rules is like calling tech support to ask them how to turn your computer on.

What's true of technology is true of English grammar: Most people use it more or less correctly without having any idea how it actually works. Those people who do know how grammar works are lovely and obsessive, and they are few and far between. They happily devote their lives to understanding the history of the Oxford comma. The rest of us just want to know how not to look foolish.

Grammar doesn't make any sense. Grammar is arbitrary and contested and political. It doesn't map onto oral speech neatly. It's hard to "hear" the difference between a colon and a comma. Reading your paper aloud doesn't help much. It might help you find where you left out a word or made other random errors, but it won't improve your grammar.

My husband used to work in tech support, so now he is the go–to guy when any one of our elderly relatives has a problem hooking up their printer. With these people he has infinite, Buddha–like patience. When I hear him on the phone talking his eighty–year–old aunt through an install of a routine software update, I fall in love with him all over again. But he knows I'm not eighty. When I have a problem, he regards me sadly, pityingly. I know what he's going to say before he even moves his mouth to form the "R."

One day I tried an experiment: I actually read the manual! It didn't solve my problem, but when I did finally beg my husband for help, he knew that I had at least tried to do this on my own. The effect of this small gesture on my part was dramatic: He fell to his knees. He suggested renewing our vows.

When you ask your instructor for help with a grammar question, your plea will be improved by showing that you have at least tried to read the manual.

What about the grammar check feature that came with your word processing program? Should you use that instead of reading the manual? It might help you see if you've left out a verb, or repeated a word. But don't accept its suggestions for rearranging sentences. Grammar check tends to apply rules without regard for sense. It also misses a lot.

You need to retain ownership of your prose. When you read a grammar manual and revise a sentence based on what you've learned, you know you're making a change for a good reason. When you click "change" in grammar check, you're rolling the dice.

Maybe you're one of those people who love to read the grammar manual. Maybe you've read several cover to cover and can tell anyone who asks the five rules of semicolon usage. That's great, but don't let it go to your head.

Remember, your college writing course is not a course in grammar. Even if your grammar is perfect, you'll still be graded primarily on whether your argument is convincing, your sources credible, and your research question engaging.

Read that manual, know that manual, and you could also start a business proofreading your friends' papers. As dorm room cottage industries go, a reliable all–night proofreading service is probably more lucrative than the black market in fake IDs. As you laugh all the way to the bank, do so with a clear conscience. Your clients failed to read the manual. They brought it on themselves.

Should I Avoid Contractions and Passive Voice?

Do you have a pet peeve? Mine is loud gum smacking and people who take up two parking spaces. But let's think for a minute about language pet peeves. Some people don't like split infinitives ("to boldly go"). Some people don't like contractions.

Go ahead and make a list of your own language pet peeves. Then read your list. Then realize that everyone you know has a list that's just as long, but completely different.

Your instructor is no exception.

Every instructor has either a written or mental list of things they hate to see in student papers. And every instructor's list is different. Think of instructors as if they were Starbucks customers: Each one likes their coffee—and their student papers—a specific way. One instructor might be a Grande–Decaf–Chai–Latte. Another one might be a Venti–Iced–Soy–Cappuccino. One instructor might be a Passive Voice–Generalizations–Split Infinitives, while another might be a

Colloquialisms–Rhetorical Questions–Wikipedia. So how do you know which is which?

Some instructors publish their preferences in their syllabi and assignments. If they announce a pet peeve ahead of time, they may be more likely to grade your paper down for ignoring it. Often, though, you discover your instructor's pet peeves only when you get your paper back.

To avoid losing points on pet peeves, imagine that you are the Starbucks barista, and your instructor has just approached the counter with assignment in hand. But rather than asking, "What can I get started for you today?" ask if there's anything in particular they don't like to see in student papers.

Chances are your instructor may be sent up the wall by at least one of the following:

- Colloquialisms (slang)
- Split infinitives ("to boldly go")
- Adverbs ("boldly")
- Sentence run—ons
- Sentence fragments
- Contractions
- Italics
- Hyper—nominalization ("utilization" instead of "use")
- Homophone screw—ups ("their," "there," and "they're"; "its" and "it's"; "to" and "too"; "your" and "you're")
- Nouns as verbs ("impact")
- Passive voice
- Citing the dictionary
- Citing Wikipedia
- Stereotypes ("Women prefer …")

- Generalizations ("In society …")
- "In conclusion …"
- Starting sentences with a preposition
- Ending sentences with a preposition
- One–word sentences
- "Etc."
- Exclamation points
- Rhetorical questions
- British spellings (if in America)
- American spellings (if in Britain)
- Use of "I," "you," or "one"
- "To be" verbs
- "Since" used as "because"
- "While" used as "although"
- No page numbers
- Serif fonts
- Sans serif fonts
- Paperclips instead of staples
- Staples instead of paperclips

As the last few pet peeves indicate, one instructor's pet peeve can be another instructor's requirement. It will not help to remind your instructor of this fact.

Pet peeves are not about correct or incorrect (though, really, get those homophones down). They are matters of preference and, as such, are not subject to outside arbitration.

Yes, it is totally unfair. But before you judge, the next time you're in a Starbucks, force yourself to walk to the counter and order just "coffee." We all have pet peeves.

My Instructor Told Me to Revise my Paper. Why?

All good papers have an evil twin: the argument built on faulty claims, the rant, the list of facts that goes nowhere. The evil twin is what happens when a writer settles for gaming the assignment. The trick to good writing is getting to know your paper's evil twin, long before it sneaks up on you. Sometimes you have to write your worst paper before you can write your best one.

I first met my paper's evil twin when I was a junior in high school. My parents, who had caught on that I was cutting class, ripped me out of public school to enroll me in a college preparatory academy. Thus I entered "Celebrity Kid High" (not its real name), attended by the likes of Brooke Shields and Anthony Bourdain. I claim no personal relationship with them, only that I know when their publicists are lying about their ages.

My public school was typical: Teachers droned on at the front of the room while kids counted the minutes until the bell. In contrast, at Celebrity Kid High, students sat in a circle rather than in rows, were asked what they thought, and were listened to when they talked. They drove nicer cars than the teachers, and I guess that gets you listened to.

To me, it was like going to Mars.

I remember the day a classmate used the word "validity" in a sentence. This kid could not have existed in my public school. Thin, sweater–vest–clad, with huge glasses that even in the hyperbolic 1980s only old people would wear—this kid would have been shoved in a locker long ago at my old school, experiencing life only through the slits in the door. He would have been too afraid to speak, much less throw around words like "validity." Funny, when I Google him now, nothing comes up but ophthalmologists.

I sat mute next to Mr. Validity for the first few months in English class, nodding as if he spoke for both of us. I couldn't wait for the first paper, on Huck Finn. If there was one area where I knew I excelled, it was writing. I expected I would get what I had been getting in my public school: an easy A.

I didn't get a grade at all. Instead, I got an invitation from the teacher, Mrs. Welk, to meet over lunch hour to "talk" about the paper. After the talk, I revised it. She read it. We met again. I revised it. She read it. We met again.

Dear Mrs. Welk, with her kind eyes and her smoker's breath, talked me through four different versions of that paper on Huck Finn before she finally accepted it for a grade. I now know that those days we met in the wood-paneled, stain-glass-windowed reading room of Celebrity Kid High, she wasn't just teaching me how to write a paper; Mrs. Welk was conducting an exorcism, conjuring and then killing off my paper's evil twin.

You can do your own exorcism at home. It's perfectly safe—even without Mrs. Welk by your side. Take whatever topic you've been working on, and conjure your good paper's evil twin. Remember, you're not creating a monster here; the power of the evil twin is that it looks a lot like the good twin, but somehow a soul is missing. Ask yourself: How could you fill the page quota with ostensibly viable sentences that convey information, yet take the reader nowhere? How many ways could you bore the reader? How could you bore yourself? When you can answer these questions, you have found your paper's evil twin.

When I ask my class to do this exercise they find it very easy to identify their paper's evil twin: It says something too obvious that everybody knows, or it gives you the facts but never makes a claim, or it gets stuck in a debate that can't be resolved. Sometimes it just fails to answer its own question.

If I could find all the drafts of my Huck Finn paper with Mrs. Welk, maybe I could learn what failing it had exhibited that took five tries to eradicate. But I guess I'll never know. I burned the evidence long ago. Or the drafts were thrown out with my retainer. Or I sold them online to aspiring plagiarists. I don't remember. Does anyone really want to remember high school?

What I do remember is the feeling of being suddenly out of my depth with a writing assignment I felt I should have aced. And I remember that a teacher sacrificed her lunch hour for weeks to make sure I wrote better. Mrs. Welk, this one's for you.

How Do I Know When I'm Done?

A paper is always done when it's due. But let's say you're sitting there with a full draft that you've worked on and revised, and the due date is still days away. How do you know your paper can't get any better? How do you know that you're done and can now move on to studying for that calculus final?

The signs that you're not done are very clear:

- Do you have trouble thinking of a title? If so, not done.
- Do your peers have trouble summarizing, in one sentence, the main point of your paper after reading it? If so, not done.
- Did your instructor or peers or tutor raise concerns about earlier drafts that your final revision does not address? If so, not done.
- Was the last time you saw your paper when you turned off your computer at the end of a five–hour writing marathon? If so, not done. Take a break and go back and proofread your work.

- Look back at the assignment. Is there an element required that you did not address? If so, not done.
- Did you learn anything from writing the paper? If not, not done.
- Did you surprise yourself by spending more time on this assignment than you thought you would? If not, not done.

Unlike the signs that you're not done, the signs that you are, in fact, done are subtle. If you miss them your paper probably won't suffer, but you may. Here are some signs that you are done:

- You changed the wording of one sentence back and forth three times. ✔ Done.
- A peer read it and said, "Wow, this is the best paper you've ever written!" And then they copied it word for word. ✔ Done.
- The librarian has run out of things to give you to read. ✔ Done.
- Your instructor has politely requested that you stop stalking them in office hours. ✔ Done.

- You are contemplating going to graduate school in this field. ✔ Done.
- Your cat has given up scratching your rug for attention and now is coughing up hairballs on your quilt. ✔ Done.

Aside from these indications, there is one less subtle, nearly foolproof sign that you are done: You hate your paper, yourself, and your life. You have lost all faith in your ability to write. You can't possibly imagine who would want to read this piece of crap. You understand that you've been an idiot to give it all your time.

Stick a fork in it. It's done.

What If Writing Never Gets Easier?

Writing never gets easier. The better you get at it, the harder it gets, because your standards get higher. But never let them get too high. Perfectionism is the enemy of writing.

My father taught me this. He hated writing. He thought he sucked at it. He was the first in his family to have more than an eighth-grade education, and he kept going until he became a professor of astronomy. He knew he wasn't dumb; he just found getting his ideas into words on paper ... hard.

Every obituary of my father has to explain why he was so very smart, but published so very little. "The great mystery," one of his colleagues told me. I had always seen my father work, so I assumed that he published what he was working on. He was, after all, a professor. I had no clue what was going on until my last year of college, when I had a chance meeting with two astronomy majors taking his class. "We love your dad's class," they told me. "He tells us all this brilliant stuff he's never even published."

"He tells you ... what now?"

The next day, I confronted my father. Walking down Amsterdam Avenue in New York toward our usual lunch (bacon and tomato grilled cheese sandwich and a chocolate shake), I asked gently, "Your students told me you teach them things you never published. Why aren't you publishing?"

My father stopped, wheeled around, and began walking in the other direction.

I called to him to come back, and he did. My father wasn't one to leave me. He would ask me nearly every day, out of every quiet moment: "Are you mad at me?" He said this as often as most parents say "I love you." And I understood it to mean the same thing.

My father kept working until he couldn't work anymore. He scribbled equations until he was taken into the hospital and, from there, to hospice. His notepads accumulated in our house, most in his office, some near his bed. After he died, my mother donated his half–finished life's work to his university's archives. The well–tailored suits he wore to the office every day were sent to the thrift store.

I miss my father. I learned so many things from him, but maybe this one is the most important to pass on: Turn off the tickertape of self–loathing in your head and press "print." Know that "good enough" is as good as it gets, as good as anyone else.

If you need to do more work to make your paper better, go ahead and do it. But if you've done everything you can and you're afraid to turn something in because you know it's not perfect, just … let it go. Turn it in, and pat yourself on the back. You did good.

Don't Forget to Thank ...

...the people who helped along the way. This author thanks Kathleen Kageff, Tim Laquintano, Carol Sickman–Garner, and John Tubbs, because whoa, this would have been a mess without them.